How to Delete Books Off Kindle

The ultimate step by step guide on how to remove books from your Kindle Device, how to manage your Kindle Account, Kindle Tips and Tricks.

<u>Disclaimer Notice:</u>

Please note the information contained within this document is for educational and entertainment purposes only. All effort has been executed to present accurate, up to date, and reliable, complete information. No warranties of any kind are declared or implied. Readers acknowledge that the author is not engaging in the rendering of legal, financial, medical or professional advice. The content within this book has been derived from various sources. Please consult a licensed professional before attempting any techniques outlined in this book.

By reading this document, the reader agrees that under no circumstances is the author responsible for any losses, direct or indirect, which are incurred as a result of the use of the information contained within this document, including, but not limited to, — errors, omissions, or inaccuracies.

TABLE OF CONTENTS

Introduction

Kindle is a small device that you use to read eBooks and it was developed by Amazon. Just as you would download music on your MP3 player or your iPod, you can download books on a Kindle and start reading. Also, just like other devices, there are several Kindle models you can purchase depending on your budget and the features you're looking for.

The more modern Kindle models come with color screens and they offer more features, like the ability to stream music and videos while maintaining the basic functions. If you want to purchase eBooks to read on your Kindle device, you can do this on the Amazon website. With Kindle, you can even download PDF files for when you need to read for your studies or your work.

Although Kindle devices are extremely portable and lightweight, you can store a huge number of eBooks on it. These devices come with a screen and a tiny keyboard allowing you to perform searches as well as other simple web-oriented actions. While most devices require a Wi-Fi connection so you can start downloading books, the newer models come with their own 3G mobile phone technology allowing you to download books no matter where you are.

In this article, we'll be going through the basics of using your Kindle device, from setting up your account to how to delete books. There's a lot to learn if you want to get the most out of your device.

How to Set Up and Manage Your Kindle Account

We are now living in the digital age where even virtual versions of books are offered to consumers. For this, the online retail giant Amazon developed Kindle, an eReader which you can use to download and read different books on a single device. If you want to start using a Kindle, the very first thing you must learn how to do is to set up your account. Setting up and managing your Kindle account are the basics. Then the longer you use your Kindle, the more you learn how to use all its features.

Tips for Setting Up Your Kindle Account

If you've purchased a brand-new Kindle device, you must first set up your account before you can start downloading books. Here are some steps for you to follow for this crucial process:

- **Join a network**

  If you purchase a Kindle device that needs a Wi-Fi connection, it's best to connect to a wireless network from the start. To do this, go to *Menu* then *Settings* then *Wi-Fi Networks*. Select your home network then enter the password if needed. You may also connect to a public Wi-Fi network if you are setting up your device in a cafe, at school or in any other public place. But when you get home, it's still a good idea to connect your Kindle to your home network. However, if your device already comes with 3G technology, you may start using it right away.

- **Register your Kindle device**

  Part of the setup process is to register your device on your existing Amazon account or create a new one. This is an easy step since the device provides on-screen prompts which you can just follow. After registering your device, you can access the Cloud feature where you will see all your stored books.

- **Connect to your social media accounts**

  Some models will ask you during the setup process if you want to connect the device to your Twitter or Facebook accounts. This is one step in the setup process which you may skip. You may also be asked if you want to add a Goodreads account where you would be given a short tutorial which contains some useful information.

  After these prompts, Kindle will also ask you to choose your preferred book genres for your personalized book suggestions. You may also opt to rate some books which you have already read to give the device an idea of what types of books you like to read.

- **Buy eBooks, download free eBooks or borrow eBooks**

The great thing about Amazon is that it has made it very easy for users to purchase books in all the available genres. If you're a fan of the classics, you can get these for free, especially if the books you want to read were published before the year 1923. This gives you over 2 million book choices!

If you want more modern titles or you're interested in browsing through the library to find a book you want, you can use your computer and head on to archive.org which is the Internet Archive. Click on *Texts* then *Browse*. Click on a title that interests you then click *Kindle* to download the file on your computer. After this, connect your Kindle using the included USB cable and simply drag the file you've downloaded to the *Documents* folder on your device.

If you own a 3G Kindle, you have the option to email the eBooks to your device. To find out the email address of your Kindle, go to *Menu* then *Settings* then *Device Options*. There, you can find the email address at the bottom of your Kindle's screen.

You can also borrow books. You can do this in two ways. First, use public libraries with Overdrive support. Though, keep in mind that this feature varies by location. Check the website of your public library to see if it has Kindle compatibility. Second, you can borrow one book each month through the Amazon Kindle Lending Library. But this feature is only available to Amazon Prime members.

- **Adjust the fonts**

Choosing a font on Kindle doesn't mean that you must stick with this font forever. Even if you don't have a preference at the beginning, it's very easy to adjust the fonts on your device. In fact, you can even adjust the fonts while you're reading. Simple tap the top part of the screen then tap on *Aa*. Then you can choose the size, style, and even the spacing of your fonts to make it easier for you to read.

Tips for Managing Your Kindle Account

After you set up your Kindle account, you can start using your device. It's also important to learn how to manage this account, especially when it comes to the most basic functions. Amazon offers its users a *Manage Your Kindle* page. On this page, you will be doing most of the work in terms of managing your account. The following are the most basic things you must know to manage your Kindle account:

- **Access the Manage Your Kindle page**

- o First, go to www.amazon.com.

- o Hover the cursor over *Your Account* for the drop-down menu to appear.

- o Select *Manage Your Kindle* then enter your login details.

- o You can also access the page directly by launching your web browser and going to www.amazon.com/manageyourkindle.

- **Managing books and documents**

This is where you can transfer books to your Kindle. Any books which you have downloaded for free, purchased or borrowed from the Kindle Store of Amazon will appear in the *Books* content library. The books which you have taken from other sources will appear in your *Personal Documents* content library.

- **Viewing books and documents**

  You can also manage the default view of
  your device. From the *Manage Your Kindle*
  page, choose the type of content you want to
  view using the drop-down *View* list. Then
  you can arrange the content by author, date
  or title by clicking on the column headers. If
  you want to see the details of a book or
  document, simply click on the plus sign
  found next to the title of the item. Finally,
  you may also search for books by entering a
  keyword on the search bar and clicking *Go*.

- **Send books and documents to your
  Kindle**

  In the same page, you also have the option
  to send your books to your Kindle or to any
  Kindle apps you have downloaded on your
  iOS or Android devices. As for the
  documents, you can only send these to your
  Kindle, not to Kindle apps. Here are the
  steps:

- Find the book or document which you want to send.

- Hover the cursor over the *Actions* list.

- Click on *Deliver to My*.

- Then choose the device from the list and click *Deliver*.

- **Changing your Kindle's email address**

  Each Kindle device comes with its own email address. But if you would like to change this, you can do this on the *Manage Your Kindle* page too:

  - Click on Personal Document Settings.

  - Find the email address you want to change then click Edit.

  - Enter your preferred email address and click Update. How to Delete a

Using Kindle, it's possible for you to download documents, magazines, and eBooks using the Amazon account that you registered as part of the initial setup process. Although these devices have the capacity to store a huge number of files, there may be times when you would want to remove some eBooks because you've already read them and you're not planning on reading them again in the future. Also, in case you lose your Kindle or it is stolen, it's recommended to remove all the files on your device. No matter what your reason is, there are a couple of ways to go about this.

Delete the Book from the Kindle App in Android and iOS Devices

The great thing about Kindle is that there are apps available for download so that you may also do your reading on your Android or iOS devices. If there comes a time when you want to remove some of your books from Kindle, you can do this using the app no matter what device you own:

- **Deleting books from the Kindle app on an Android device**

  o On an Android device, the app comes with a 5-way controller. Use this button to delete the book.

  o Find the book that you are planning to delete from the *Home* screen on your Kindle library.

  o Once there, tap the toggle on the left of the 5-way controller.

  o Tap *Remove from Device* then tap the middle of the 5-way controller.

- **Deleting books from the Kindle app on an iOS device**

  o First, you must login to the online library on the website of Amazon then go to the *Content and Device* page.

o Tap on the *Your Content* tab for a list of your books.

o Tap on the *Select* option so that each row gets an empty box which you check to select.

o At the top-left side of your Kindle's screen, find the *Delete* button and tap on it.

o You'll get prompted to confirm your choice. Tap *Yes, Delete Permanently* after checking that you've selected the correct book.

o Sync your iOS device with your Kindle account. For this step, tap on the *Kindle* icon to open the Kindle application.

o Find the three dots located on the

upper-right-hand corner of the screen then select the option *Sync & Check for Items*. Doing this removes the books from your account as well.

Delete the Book from the Content Library

Another method to delete a book from your device is to remove it from your Kindle's content library. Here are the steps for this:

- Open the content library of your Kindle.

- Search for the book that you are planning to remove. For this method, you have two options: to archive the book or to delete it.

- Once you've found the title of the book that you plan to delete, swipe left then tap the *Archive* button. This places the book in your

Kindle Archive without deleting it. This means that it won't appear in your Kindle Library, but the book doesn't get deleted.

- You can also tap and hold on the cover of the book for one second for the menu to appear.

- Tap *Remove from Device* to delete the book.

It's important to note that Amazon keeps a record of all the content you have purchased. This information is kept in your account with Amazon. This account allows you to sync the books you've downloaded across all your devices which have Kindle apps. Even if you delete a book from your devices, this doesn't mean that it also gets deleted from your purchase library on the cloud servers of Amazon. So, you can download it again free of charge if you need to.

Delete the Book Permanently Through Your Computer

You also have the choice to delete the book entirely even from your Amazon cloud library. People typically do this when their Kindle gets stolen or when they lose their device. For this method, you need a computer or laptop. Then follow these steps:

- On your Amazon account page, navigate to *Manage Your Content and Devices*.

- Go to *Books* and find the book title that you would like to delete. If you've purchased and downloaded lots of books, you can use the *Sort By* option to find the one you need faster.

- When you've located the book title that you would like to remove, click on the ... button. You can find this on the left side of the book's title.

- After clicking, a pop-up window will appear where you click on *Delete*.

- You'll get another prompt which warns you that if you delete the item, you're also removing it permanently from your Kindle Library.

This means that if you need to read the book again, you must purchase it from Amazon. Therefore, you must make sure that you really want to delete the book from your account before you perform all these steps.

Kindle Tips and Tricks

After learning the basics, you shouldn't stop there. The great thing about Kindle is that there are so many tips, tricks, and hacks you can do to get the most out of your device. Just like any other device, Kindle comes with plenty of features. Sadly, most people who use Kindle stop at the basics. As long as they're able to download books and manage their settings, they feel satisfied.

But if you would like to learn more about your Kindle, this last section of the article will help you out. Here, we'll be going through some of the most useful tips and tricks. The more you learn about your Kindle, the more you're unlocking its potential.

How to Take Screenshots

There may be times when you need to take a

snapshot of the device's settings page, you would like to share a piece of text from the book you're reading or share an image with someone from a document on your Kindle. Whatever your reason is for needing a screenshot, the good news is that taking screenshots is possible on most models. Here's how you can take screenshots on different Kindle devices:

- **Kindle Paperwhite:** Touch two opposite corners on the screen simultaneously. Once you see a flash, this indicates that you've successfully taken a screenshot which gets stored in your device's root folder. To get the screenshot, you should connect your device to a computer using the USB cable. This applies to most Kindle devices too.

- **Kindle (Kindle Touch):** Press then hold the device's *Home* button then tap on its screen.

- **Kindle Keyboard (Kindle DX or Kindle 3):** On the keyboard, press *Alt-*

Shift-G to take a screenshot.

- **Kindle 4:** Press the *Keyboard* and *Home* buttons simultaneously then release to take a screenshot.

- **Kindle Fire HD and Kindle Fire 2:** Press then hold the power along with the volume down simultaneously to take a screenshot. For these models, you can access the screenshots from the *Photos* app.

- **Older models of Kindle Fire (those which don't have volume buttons):** The bad news is, if you own such models, it's a bit more challenging to take screenshots, but it's not impossible! Just connect the device to your computer. Just make sure you install Kindle SDK first so that you may take a screenshot using the development environment.

- **Kindle App (on different devices):** Since the app itself doesn't come with a screenshot function, you must take the screenshot the same way you would on the device you're using.

Increasing Your Battery

If you don't want your device to turn off in the middle of reading, then this is one trick you should definitely learn and use. Although most of the time you would have access to power outlets so you can keep reading continuously, there may be times when you have to take a trip where you won't be able to charge your Kindle's battery. In this case, it's useful to learn how to increase your battery life. Here are some tips:

- **Make sure that the firmware of your Kindle is always updated**

    There are times when Kindle becomes susceptible to bugs, some of which can affect your device's battery life. For instance, one such bug which ate up battery life was an issue with Kindle indexing books and the device was not able to fall asleep properly. To avoid these issues, make sure that your firmware is always up-to-date.

- **Turn off the radio**

Overall, Kindle is an excellent eReader because it's so efficient, but there are some features of this device which make the battery drain a lot faster than it should such as 3G and Wi-Fi radios. So, if you don't need to connect to a network, it's better to turn these off if you would like to save your battery.

- **Turn down the backlight**

This tip doesn't apply to all Kindle devices because some of them don't have backlighting. But if the device you own does, you may want to turn down the backlight, especially during the day when you don't need it.

- **Disable the automatic page refresh feature**

A lot of people find this feature to be highly convenient. But if you would like to increase the life of your battery, you should turn this feature off. Then simply refresh the page occasionally when you need to.

- **Put your device to sleep manually**

Just like most Kindle users out there, you may rely on the automatic sleep function of the device. But it's much more energy efficient if you manually put your device to sleep right after you finish using it. This means that it stops using energy right away instead of having to wait for a period of time before falling asleep.

- **If you want to add books, do this while charging**

Each time you download an eBook to your device, the operating system indexes it. Unfortunately, this process is a very intense one and the more books you download, the longer this process will take. Indexing is another cause for a shortened battery life. So, if you plan to add books, especially if you plan to add a lot at a time, plug your device in first so it won't run out of battery while it's indexing.

- **Take care of the battery**

It's also important for you to take care of your battery. For one, keep the device at room temperature all the time, never in places with extreme temperatures. When you're charging the device, make sure to charge it properly. Never leave it charging for a long time, even after it's fully charged. Also, you shouldn't pull out the charger when the device isn't fully charged yet.

Change the Settings

The more you explore your Kindle, the more you'll learn about it. After you've mastered the basics, you may now want to customize it according to your own preferences. Changing the settings of your Kindle is one of the easiest things you can do. Here are the steps for this:

- Tap the *Menu* button to get the drop-down box located in the upper corner of your screen.

- Navigate to and select *Settings* using your device's 5-way controller.

- Check which setting you plan to change. This is where you can change anything you want on your device's settings to customize it.

- When you're done making changes, tap the *Home* button.

Set a Passcode

If you want to increase the privacy level of your device, all you have to do is set a passcode on it. This is another easy trick to employ and it's very useful, especially if you don't want other people to snoop around on your Kindle. Follow these steps to set a passcode and cancel it:

- **Setting the passcode**

    - On the *Home* screen, tap on *Menu* then *Settings* then Device *Options* then *Device Passcode*.

    - When the window pops up, you need to type in the passcode twice.

    - Tap *OK*.

  Here's a useful hint for you: If you forget things easily, you may want to jot down a clue for your passcode on the protective case of your device where it won't be easily seen.

- **Canceling the passcode**

  o On the Home screen, tap on Menu then Settings then Device Options then Device Passcode.

  o Then tap on Turn Off Passcode.

  o When the window pops up, you must first input the passcode you've set so confirm this action.

Force Restart

Our final tip is how to force restart your Kindle when you're experiencing issues with it. This tip is very useful when your Kindle freezes and you don't know what else to do. There are two ways to do this:

- **Soft Reset**

This method restarts your device without having an effect on the data. You may do a soft reset if your Kindle isn't responding or if it gets frozen. Here are the steps:

- **For 1st to 4th Generation Kindle models:** Press the *Power* button and hold it for up to 20 seconds or until your device turns off.

- **For 5th to 7th Generation Kindle models:** Press the *Volume Down* and *Power* buttons at the same time and hold for about 10 seconds or until your device turns off.

- **Hard Reset**

This method has a bigger impact on your device, so you must think about whether you want to do it first. When you perform a hard reset on your Kindle, this brings the device back to its factory default settings.

This means that it may clear all the data from your device's memory. If you think that you have no choice but to perform a hard reset, follow these steps for 3rd to 7th Generation Kindle models:

- o First, make sure that your device has at least a 30% battery level.

- o For the first option, navigate to Settings then *Device Options* then *Reset to Factory Defaults* then *Reset*.

- o For the second option, turn the device off first. Then simultaneously press and hold the *Volume Down* and *Power* buttons.

- o After doing this, the system recovery screen of Amazon will appear. On this screen, select *Wipe Data/Factory Reset*.

o Find to this selection using the *Volume* buttons and click on the selection using the *Power* button.

o Select *Yes - Delete All User Data* by pressing the *Power* button.

Conclusion

Amazon's Kindle is a revolutionary device. It's obvious that this incredible eReader has forever changed how we read books. Now we don't have to carry heavy books with us wherever we go. All we have to do is purchase, download or borrow them and store all our books on a single device. Although there may be other good types of eReaders out there, if you're looking to purchase one, you may still opt for a Kindle. If you've recently purchased such a device, you now know that there's a lot more to it than just the basic features.

When you learn all the basic features of Kindle, you will be able to use it adequately. You will be able to perform all the basic functions such as downloading books and reading them. But if you'd like to get the most out of your device, the best thing to do is to learn everything that you can about it. In this article, we've discussed several tips and tricks which can help you from the time you set up your account. Keep using your Kindle and you may discover new things and new features which you never even knew existed!

www.ingramcontent.com/pod-product-compliance
Lightning Source LLC
Chambersburg PA
CBHW051217050326
40689CB00008B/1350